DINOSAUR DAYS
SPINOSAURUS

HEIGHT: 20' (6.1 M)

HEIGHT: 5' (1.5 M)

DINOSAUR DAYS
SPINOSAURUS

SARA GILBERT

CREATIVE EDUCATION CREATIVE PAPERBACKS

Table of Contents

DINOSAUR DAYS — **Spinosaurus**

Published by Creative Education
and Creative Paperbacks
P.O. Box 227, Mankato,
Minnesota 56002
Creative Education and Creative
Paperbacks are imprints of
The Creative Company
www.thecreativecompany.us

Book design by Blue Design
(www.bluedes.com)
Art direction by Rita Marshall
Printed in the United States of America

Photographs by Alamy (Mohamad
Haghani), Creative Commons
Wikimedia (Mike Bowler/Flickr,
Mariomassone, Steveoc 86, Ernst
Stromer), Thinkstock (anankkml,
chronicler101, dottedhippo,
Elenarts, Gluiki, homeworks255,
leonello, LindaMarieB, MR1805,
rikkyal, Vac1, Warpaintcobra)

6

Library of Congress Cataloging-
in-Publication Data
Names: Gilbert, Sara, author.
Title: Spinosaurus / Sara Gilbert.
Series: Dinosaur days.
Includes bibliographical
references and index.
Summary: This introductory
exploration uncovers the discovery
of *Spinosaurus* fossils before
revealing information about its
era, features, and lifestyle, as
well as its eventual extinction.
Identifiers: ISBN 978-1-64026-
048-1 (hardcover) / ISBN 978-
1-62832-636-9 (pbk) / ISBN
978-1-64000-164-0 (eBook)

This title has been submitted for CIP
processing under LCCN 2018938975.

CCSS: RI.1.1, 2, 4, 5, 6, 7; RI.2.1, 2, 5, 6,
7; RI.3.1, 2, 5, 7; RF.1.1, 3, 4; RF.2.3, 4

First Edition HC 9 8 7 6 5 4 3 2 1
First Edition PBK 9 8 7 6 5 4 3 2 1

Meet *Spinosaurus*!

Welcome to the National Geographic Museum. We are in Washington, D.C. We have one of the only *Spinosaurus* **skeletons** in the world. We love to share it with people!

National Geographic's Spinosaurus *is part of an exhibition that travels the world.*

paleontologist:
pay-lee-on-TOL-o-gist

Found and Lost

Ernst Stromer was a
paleontologist. He found the
first *Spinosaurus* **fossils** in 1912
in Egypt. He took them to a
museum in Germany. But the
bones were destroyed during
World War II.

IN THE WATER, *SPINOSAURUS* PADDLED WITH ITS FEET AND MOVED ITS LONG TAIL FROM SIDE TO SIDE.

Splashing Around

Spinosaurus lived in northern Africa with other giant dinosaurs such as *Carcharodontosaurus*. That area is now the Sahara Desert. But during the Cretaceous period, there were lots of rivers for *Spinosaurus* to swim in!

Carcharodontosaurus: kar-kar-o-DON-tuh-SAWR-us

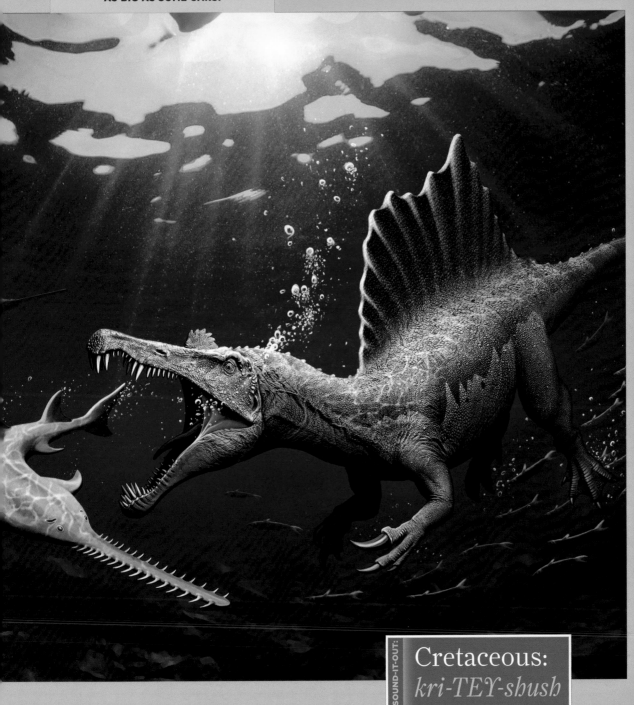

THE FISH *SPINOSAURUS* CAUGHT WERE AS BIG AS SOME CARS!

SOUND-IT-OUT:

Cretaceous:
kri-TEY-shush

SPINOSAURUS HAD INTERLOCKING, CONE-SHAPED TEETH—SIMILAR TO A CROCODILE'S.

River Monster

Spinosaurus was huge! It could have been more than 50 feet (15.2 m) long. It may have weighed up to 20 tons (18.1 t). That was bigger than *Tyrannosaurus rex*! Its teeth were long and sharp.

Spinosaurus had a sail on its back. The sail could be seven feet (2.1 m) tall! It stuck out of the water as *Spinosaurus* swam.

227 MILLION YEARS AGO
LATE TRIASSIC

205 MILLION YEARS AGO
EARLY JURASSIC

180 MILLION YEARS AGO
MID-JURASSIC

Timeline

SPINOSAURUS LIVED HERE!

159 MILLION YEARS AGO
LATE JURASSIC

144 MILLION YEARS AGO
EARLY CRETACEOUS

98 MILLION YEARS AGO
LATE CRETACEOUS

coelacanths:
SEEL-uh-kanths

Hungry Hunter

Scientists think *Spinosaurus* spent a lot of time in the water. Dense bones helped it float. On land, it may have walked on two legs or on all four.

Spinosaurus ate a lot. We think its favorite meal was fish. It caught **coelacanths**, sawfish, and sharks that swam in rivers.

Stromer drew the Spinosaurus *fossils before the remains were sent to Germany.*

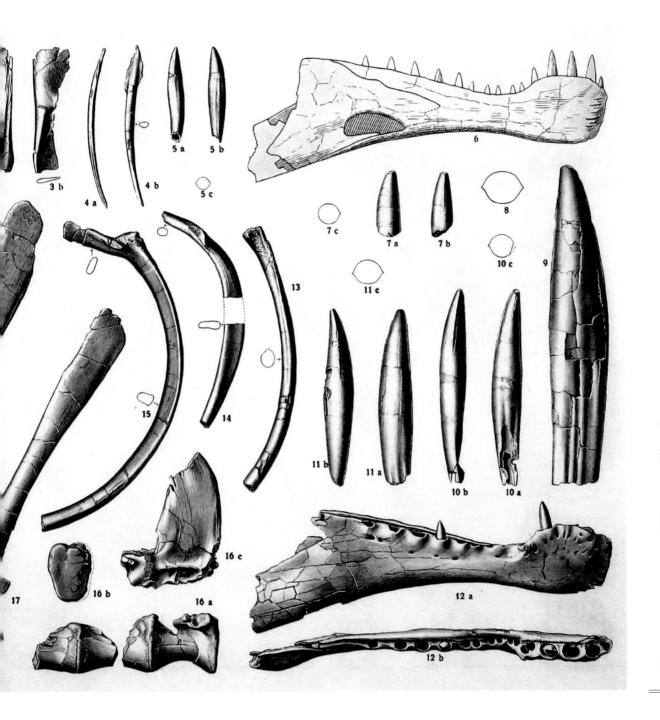

SPINOSAURUS IS THE LARGEST KNOWN MEAT-EATING DINOSAUR.

All Dried Up

No one knows how *Spinosaurus* died out. Maybe as the **climate** changed, it got too hot. Rivers dried up, and fish disappeared. Scientists hope to find more clues about this dinosaur in the future!

Glossary

climate — the weather conditions in an area over a period of time

coelacanths — large, bony fish more closely related to land animals than to most fish

fossils — bones or plants preserved for millions of years

paleontologist — a scientist who studies fossils

skeletons — the bones that support bodies

Read More

Gregory, Josh. *Spinosaurus.* Ann Arbor, Mich.: Cherry Lake, 2014.

West, David. *Spinosaurus: The Thorn Lizard.* New York: PowerKids Press, 2012.

Websites

DK Find Out!: Spinosaurus
https://www.dkfindout.com/us/dinosaurs-and-prehistoric-life/dinosaurs/spinosaurus/
See a diagram of *Spinosaurus*, and take a dinosaur quiz!

National Geographic Kids: Spinosaurus
https://kids.nationalgeographic.com/animals/Spinosaurus/#Spinosaurus.jpg
Read more about *Spinosaurus* and other dinosaurs!